500
Reasons
Why You're
My Best
Friend

Other Books
by Lorraine Bodger

. . . .

Crazy About You

511 Things Only Women Understand

2,001 Ways to Pamper Yourself

For You, My Friend, I Wish . . .

For Your Birthday, I Wish . . .

500 Reasons Why You're My Best Friend

Lorraine Bodger

BARNES
&NOBLE
BOOKS
NEW YORK

Published by MJF Books
Fine Communications
322 Eighth Avenue
New York, NY 10001

500 Reasons Why You're My Best Friend
Library of Congress Catalog Card Number 2003108257
ISBN 1-56731-597-6

Illustrations by Lorraine Bodger
Book design by Lisa Martin

VB 10 9 8 7 6 5 4 3 2

Introduction

✳

Women are incredibly lucky: We have best girl-friends. They hold us together through good times and bad. They keep us sane. They keep us talking. They keep us in touch with our feelings. From the time we're in our strollers to the time we're using walkers, best friends are a crucial part of female culture. Guys may supply the electricity in our lives, but girls supply the grounding.

No one has to tell *you* how important your best friend is. You couldn't live without her. Other relationships may come and go, you may get married, you may be on the outs with your family—but your best friend is forever. Thank heaven. You can call her in a crisis or for no reason at all. You can see her every day or only every now and then. It doesn't matter when, why, or how often you're together—she's your best friend and you love her. She loves you, too, and there's no other friendship in the world that works quite as well as this one. You depend on each other as you depend on no one else, and life would be pretty tough without her. Actually, life would be impossible without her because your days aren't complete unless the two of you can hash them over in every detail by phone or e-mail or in person. Nothing is too large or too small to tackle with your best friend, and some things don't even feel real until you share them with her. She takes your emotional temperature, and you do the same for her. It's been that way for years, and there's no reason to think it won't go on that way for quite a few more.

So what's it all about, anyway? It might be hard for a man to understand why you and your best friend are so involved with each other, but no woman would question it for a moment. Your best friend is your confidante, your buddy, your playmate, your biggest supporter, and sometimes your biggest critic. She *might* be your real sister, but even if she's not, she's your sister in spirit. There are a multitude of reasons why she's your best friend, and here are five hundred of them for you to celebrate.

500 Reasons Why You're My Best Friend

• 1 •

I can tell you anything,
and you won't be shocked.

• 2 •

I love listening to your stories.

• 3 •

When I'm a little down
you make me laugh.

· 4 ·

When I'm *really* down
you cry with me.

· 5 ·

Remember that time I tripped and
fell in front of all those people?
You were the first one there to help
me up and dust me off.

· 6 ·

You let me stay overnight
when my toilet was backed up
and the plumber couldn't get
to my house for two days.

· 7 ·

You can keep your cool in any
emergency, even the ones involving guys.

· 8 ·

If I have to, I can call you
at three in the morning. And you
know you can call me, too.

· 9 ·

You loaned me your best cashmere
sweater for my Most Important Date.

· 10 ·

You gave me a Tampax
when I needed one in the
worst possible way.

· 11 ·

You brought over your
computer when mine went
belly-up the day before my
master's thesis was due.

· 12 ·

You took care of my kids when I had
to rush my mother to the hospital.

· 13 ·

We went to all the great
rock concerts together.

· 14 ·

We love the same movies.
Some of the same movies.
Well, the important ones, for sure.

• 15 •

Sometimes you call me
at exactly the moment
I'm thinking of you.

• 16 •

You were my bridal attendant
and I was yours.

• 17 •

You threw my first baby shower.

· 18 ·

You helped me
a. cut my hair
b. color my hair
c. streak my hair
d. straighten my hair
e. all of the above

· 19 ·

Your advice is sensible,
reliable, and caring.
You think the same of mine.

· 20 ·

When I moved into my new
house, you helped me unpack.
And unpack and unpack.

· 21 ·

You bring me tomatoes
from your garden.

· 22 ·

We stayed up all night together
watching reruns of *Star Trek.*

· 23 ·

I'd trust you with my life, and
you'd trust me with yours.

· 24 ·

Yours was the first call
I got on my new cell phone.

· 25 ·

You took me to have my ears
pierced and let me hold your
hand during the whole thing.

· 26 ·

You went with me when
I bought my first pair
of contact lenses.

· 27 ·

When I was terribly unhappy
at my job, you encouraged
me to apply for a new one
and took me out to celebrate
when I landed it.

· 28 ·

We visited each other at college
and went on bad double dates.
We still laugh about it.

· 29 ·

We went to Europe together
and had the time of our lives.

· 30 ·

You sent me CARE packages
when I was in the Peace Corps.

· 31 ·

We loved all the same children's books.

· 32 ·

You cooked vegetarian meals for me
when I was going through a stage, and
I cooked diet meals for you when
you were trying to lose five pounds.

· 33 ·

We have private jokes.

· 34 ·

You took me for dozens of walks
when I broke up with my boyfriend,
and you listened with your heart.

· 35 ·

The two of us worked out
together at home until we felt
fit enough to join the gym.

· 36 ·

You didn't mind when I won the swim meet, and I didn't mind when you won the tennis match. (Okay, I minded a little, but only because I'm green with envy for your backhand.)

· 37 ·

A brand-new manicure, we totally agree, is the perfect picker-upper when life is looking gray and gloomy.

· 38 ·

I take pleasure in your competence.

· 39 ·

I'm safe in your hands: You'd
never let me buy a pair of
pants that looked hideous on me.

· 40 ·

You're an incredible source of
information about everything from
vacuum cleaners to gynecologists.

· 41 ·

You always, always saved me a
seat in the high school cafeteria.

· 42 ·

When I got a tattoo, you
barely blinked an eye.

· 43 ·

Together we obsess about our

a. thighs

b. sex lives

c. biological clocks

d. mothers

e. careers

f. all of the above

· 44 ·

You know how to remove
any stain in the universe.

· 45 ·

When I freaked out at my child's
second birthday party, you stepped
right in and took over while I went
and screamed in a closet.

· 46 ·

You got high heels before
I did, but I got
a bikini before
you did.

· 47 ·

I taught you how to drive,
and you taught me how to knit.

· 48 ·

You rushed out to pick
me up when I had a really
horrible date who left me
stranded at a restaurant
ten miles out of town.

· 49 ·

Our husbands actually
like each other, so the four
of us can go out together.
A miracle.

· 50 ·

We have matching
stretch marks.

500 Reasons Why You're My Best Friend

· 51 ·

I know your moods
so well that I know exactly
when to press you to tell
me what's wrong—and when
to leave you in peace.

· 52 ·

You're honest, but tactful.
Usually.

· 53 ·

You're the first person I'd
call if I needed

a. a reality check

b. a short-term loan

c. help solving a family problem

d. an ally in a fight for a good cause

e. a shoulder to cry on

· 54 ·

If I'm way out of line,
you tell me. And when
I'm doing a good job,
you tell me that, too.

· 55 ·

Your stamina for
shopping is *awesome*.

· *56* ·

We spend Christmas Eve
together whenever we're in
the same city. We've been
doing it for aeons.

· 57 ·

Screening my phone
calls *never* means
screening *your* call.

· 58 ·

We can bounce ideas
off each other and talk them
through until they either
make sense or go away.

· 59 ·

We went to different colleges
and we didn't know how we
were going to survive the
separation—but it only made
our friendship stronger.

· 60 ·

We went to the same
college, and you always
shared your goody bags
from home with me.

· 61 ·

I met you at the airport when you
left your first husband. You gave me
a divorce shower when I left mine.

· 62 ·

You helped me get through my

a. thirtieth birthday

b. fortieth birthday

c. fiftieth birthday

d. sixtieth birthday

e. all of the above

· 63 ·

You introduced me to decaf
cappuccino with a sprinkling of
cinnamon on top. I introduced
you to margaritas.

· *64* ·

We helped each other
torture our siblings. How
much fun was *that?*

· *65* ·

You think I'm smart, capable,
clever, and pretty. You're my
one-woman cheering section.

· 66 ·

You don't expect me to be
Superwoman—you know and
accept my limitations.

· 67 ·

The two of us actually changed a
flat tire together. (It took us three
hours and we yelled at each other
a lot, but hey, we did it!)

· 68 ·

Discussing the intricacies
of underwear for hours on end
is one of our favorite pastimes.

· 69 ·

Discussing the nuances of color
for hours on end is another. You
understand perfectly the differences
between flame, scarlet, cherry,
cerise, cardinal, garnet, ruby,
rose, berry, and carmine.

· 70 ·

You don't get mad if I'm wildly
busy and don't have time for
a long conversation.

· 71 ·

You redid my makeup for
me when it was starting
to look old-fashioned.

· 72 ·

If the movie gets scary, you
let me know when it's safe
to open my eyes and take
my hands away from my ears.

· 73 ·

Whatever each of us may
have ordered, we always split
the bill right down the middle.
We both know it will all
work out in the end.

· 74 ·

In any crunch, you back me up.

· 75 ·

When you were eight months pregnant
and feeling like a whale, I told you
you looked radiant. You *did* look radiant.

· 76 ·

You venture into new
technology with excitement
instead of trepidation.

· 77 ·

The minute I hear your voice
on the phone, I cheer up.

· 78 ·

You loathe mice
as much as I do.

· 79 ·

We saved each other's sanity
when we were both stuck at
home with toddlers. All it took
was fifteen phone calls a day.

· 80 ·

I wouldn't reveal that
incredibly idiotic remark
I made to my boss to
anyone else but you.

• 81 •

You don't care about

   a. football

   b. oil filters

   c. crabgrass

   d. megahertz

   e. single malts

   f. trout streams

any more than I do, but we let
our men ramble on about them.

· 82 ·

You're the only person I know who
actually *accomplishes* each day
what she sets out to *do* each day.
How on earth do you manage it?

· 83 ·

When things go bad, get stuck,
or stop being fun, you repeat your
motto: Change your thinking
and move on. I love that.

· 84 ·

The big meeting was ten minutes
away when I tore a gigantic hole
in the knee of my panty hose.
You didn't miss a beat: You towed
me to the ladies' room, pulled
your panty hose off, and gave
them to me. The meeting was
a smashing success.

· 85 ·

We both love our mothers-in-law.

· 86 ·

We both hate our
mothers-in-law.

· 87 ·

You insisted I get rid of my
bread machine, pasta maker,
waffle iron, deep fryer, ice cream
maker, hibachi, juice extractor,
and complete set of spice
grinders. What a relief not to
have to be Superchef anymore.

· 88 ·

Juicy gossip is juicier
when I share it with you.

· 89 ·

Your daughter was the flower
girl at my wedding. She looked
just like a miniature *you!*

· 90 ·

We understand finances: Saving
is buying two of something if it's
on sale. Credit is buying things
without worrying about paying
for them. An ATM withdrawal
is money that doesn't count.
Check stubs are merely rough,
general outlines of our bank
accounts. Just joking.

· 91 ·

You're patient with me
when I'm stuck on a guy and
can't stop talking about him.

· 92 ·

You send me postcards
when you're traveling.

· 93 ·

We joined Fat Busters
together. We took off the
weight and we kept it off.
We are *totally amazing*.

· 94 ·

Sometimes we're under a lot
of stress and we snap at each
other. Look, these things happen
between friends. We get past it.

· 95 ·

In sixth grade we had
crushes on the same boy,
but you let me have him.

· 96 ·

In tenth grade we had
crushes on the same boy,
and I let you have him.

· 97 ·

Remember the time we rode
our bikes way beyond the next
town, got lost, and couldn't find our
way back home until nine at night?
(Our folks had called the cops, and
we were grounded for two days.)

· 98 ·

You send me encouraging
e-mails at critical moments,
and I send them to you, too.

· 99 ·

Your cat is my favorite cat,
and my dog is your favorite
dog. Too bad the cat and
the dog don't like each other.

· 100 ·

Shh, don't tell anyone:
We secretly read bodice-rippers.

· 101 ·

Even when our schedules are
completely out of sync we
manage to shake out an hour
for a cup of tea
together.

· 102 ·

Your spice jars are not
alphabetized. Your books are not
arranged according to size and
color. The towels in your linen
closet are not perfectly stacked.
Your shoes have no shoe trees
stuck in them. In short, you're
not a paragon of meticulous
organization who would make me
feel like a total shlump. Bless you.

· 103 ·

You don't get uptight
or irritated when I

a. talk

b. yell

c. laugh

d. sing

e. cheer

much too loudly.

· 104 ·

You would never, ever say to me,
"Don't wear those fabulous bright
red high heels with the strap across
the instep because they'll throw off
your posture and ruin your ankles."

· 105 ·

We take turns trying new wrinkle
creams. And we'll keep trying
until we find one that works.

· 106 ·

You introduced me
to karaoke. I'm not sure
that was a favor.

· 107 ·

When we're feeling unappreciated
by our mates and a little restless
around the edges, we go to a bar
and flirt with the bartender.
That sure does the trick.

· 108 ·

The hunt for a perfect pair
of jeans has been a key
theme of our friendship.

· 109 ·

You stop me firmly when
I start apologizing for things
that aren't my fault.

· 110 ·

You bring your problems
to me and let me help
you solve them.

· 111 ·

I can ask you for a favor
and I know you'll do it if
you possibly can. You know
you can ask me, too.

· 112 ·

For years we've discussed and
debated every kind of birth
control—pills, diaphragms,
condoms, the whole enchilada.

· 113 ·

You helped me turn my mattress
when there was no hulking man
around to help me do it.

· 114 ·

You carted off the Giant
Zucchini that was threatening
to take over
my garden.

· 115 ·

Your diamond earrings were
my "something borrowed"
when I got married. Their
sparkle helped *me* sparkle.

· 116 ·

We screamed at
horror movies together
in the eighth grade.

· 117 ·

We cried at romantic movies
together in the ninth grade.

· 118 ·

We yawned at foreign movies
together in the tenth grade.

· 119 ·

We made our *own* movie
together in the eleventh grade.

· 120 ·

The timing was awful: Your
husband was on a business trip
when you went into labor, so
I went through the whole birth
with you. You were fantastic
and I didn't do too badly myself.
Talk about bonding . . .

· 121 ·

You took my entire family into
your home when that terrible
storm forced us out of our house.
And you made it feel like a great
big three-day party.

· 122 ·

We don't look alike and we don't
sound alike—but we think alike
about all the important things,
and that's what counts.

· 123 ·

You're irreverent
and mischievous, and
your giggles are infectious.

· 124 ·

You make room for me in
your life, even when your
life is crowded and busy.

· 125 ·

I'm not embarrassed
to cry in front of you.

· 126 ·

So many people get bent out
of shape when a friend makes
a big life change, but not you.
You're there, encouraging me
and cheering me on.

· 127 ·

You keep in touch with friends
from the past. Which gives
me confidence that you'll
always keep in touch with me.

· 128 ·

I admire your self-control:
You actually think
before you speak.

· 129 ·

At work you taught me
the ropes—how to use

a. the brand-new copier

b. the weird phone system

c. the complicated spreadsheets

d. the vending machine that makes
undrinkable coffee

e. the broken tampon dispenser in
the ladies' room

I wouldn't have lasted
a week without you.

· 130 ·

When we go to the movies you
always buy the Extra-Large
Super-Giant Tub-o'-Popcorn,
and you share.

· 131 ·

You have courage, even when
you're afraid. (Sometimes, to
get through a tough situation,
I sort of pretend I'm you.)

· 132 ·

I appreciate how you ferret out
my secrets when I really want
to tell them to you but can't
quite bring myself to do it.

· 133 ·

You have seventy-five
pairs of shoes and you
don't feel guilty about it.

· 134 ·

Life is too short, we agree,
to stay mad at each other
for more than a day at a time.
Well, maybe two days.

· 135 ·

It takes a full-blown crisis to
bring out the best in some people.
Not you—you're at your best
every day. Most days.

· 136 ·

It's odd, but your husband
is actually a lot like me,
and mine is a lot like you.

· 137 ·

My day goes better
when I know that dinner
with you is waiting to
happen at the end of it.

· *138* ·

I can listen to you sing
off-key. But not for too long.

· *139* ·

No one else gives me
the total attention you do,
when I have a problem
or I just need to talk.

· 140 ·

You notice when I'm in
pain, psychic or physical.

· 141 ·

You were always terrific at
explaining the unexplainable, like

a. calculus

b. football

c. mortgages

d. computer programs

e. why men leave

· 142 ·

I've never felt that any of our
arguments or disagreements
would end our friendship.

· 143 ·

If I'm telling you something I *think*
is important, and it's actually
complete nonsense, somehow
I start to hear it through your
ears. That turns me around fast!

· 144 ·

You never forget to send me
a birthday card. I'm lying—
you did forget at least twice,
but who's counting?

· 145 ·

You've grown into your looks,
and you're more beautiful now
than when we were young.

· 146 ·

You taught me the most
important thing about desk
work: Make piles (to feel
organized) and ignore piles
(until most of the stuff in them
becomes obsolete).
A life lesson.

· 147 ·

When I moved into my postdivorce
apartment, you gave me the perfect
gift: a set of crisp new sheets and
pillowcases, a fluffy new quilt, and
a beautiful bedspread, so my
bedroom could be my refuge.

· 148 ·

In high school, we used our
baby-sitting earnings to pay for our own
telephones so we could talk to each
other endlessly without driving our
parents completely around the bend.

· 149 ·

You taught me Rule No. 1
about clothes shopping:
If it looks sensational, buy two.

· 150 ·

You taught me Rule No. 2
about clothes shopping:
After thirty, buy quality items
and leave the cheap flash
to the teenagers.

· 151 ·

You taught me Rule No. 3 about
clothes shopping: 85 percent
of what you buy will be mistakes.

· 152 ·

We had total makeovers together.
(We barely recognized each other after
The Experts were through with us.)

· 153 ·

When I crashed onto my knee
and had to walk with a cane for six
weeks, you came every Wednesday
to help me hobble to the local café
for a delicious espresso and a slice
of Italian cheesecake. I know for a
fact that you helped me heal faster.

· 154 ·

We learned double Dutch
together. Fell on our behinds
together a few times, too.

· 155 ·

When we're old and gray we'll
still be calling each other
three times a day to keep
up with breaking news.

· 156 ·

You always let me know if

a. my scale is <u>l</u>ying to me

b. my hair stylist is <u>l</u>ying to me

c. the guy I'm interested
in is <u>l</u>ying to me

d. my boss is <u>l</u>ying to me

e. my mother is <u>l</u>ying to me

· 157 ·

Remember the year we had
a lemonade stand in front
of your house? We were
best friends even then.

· 158 ·

If I have to go out of town
on business, you pick up my mail
for me and check on the plants,
too. You're the only one I trust
with the key to my house.

· 159 ·

We both almost had nervous
breakdowns when our teenagers
first got their driving licenses.

· 160 ·

When I'm procrastinating
hopelessly, you give me the
push I need to get going.

· 161 ·

You encourage me to be
as good to myself as
I am to everyone else.

· 162 ·

You never tease me in
front of other people.

· 163 ·

Your pancake breakfasts
are the best in the world.

· 164 ·

I love how you bring
new people into my life.

· 165 ·

You never pretend to be
someone you're not. You always
say, What you see is what you get.
I always say, Amen to that.

· 166 ·

We mentor each other.

· 167 ·

You come up with interesting
things to do when we take
an afternoon off for fun.

· 168 ·

You remind me, when I have
to make choices, that it's my life
and nobody else's, that I can do
whatever I want, and that in the
end I don't have to justify my
behavior to anyone but myself.
Another life lesson.

· 169 ·

When I'm rushed off my feet,
you pick up milk, bread, and
whatever else I need at the
supermarket when you do your
own shopping. And you leave
the bag at my door without
even waiting for a thank-you.

· *170* ·

At Christmas, we have
a ball wrapping gifts,
baking cookies, and trimming
our trees together.

· 171 ·

You're the only one who
can beat me at Scrabble.
But I'm the only one who
can beat you at Monopoly.

· 172 ·

We drove cross-country
together, just for the fun of it.
Wow, what an unbelievable
trip that was.

· 173 ·

When my back
went out, you took me to
your chiropractor.

· 174 ·

When I had a terrible
migraine, you dashed to
the pharmacy to get
my prescription filled.

· 175 ·

You know my dark side and
I know yours. No judgments.

· 176 ·

Some things are just plain more
fun when we do them together.
Like eating junk food.

· 177 ·

You overheard (eavesdropped on?) the boss praising my work, and you ran like the wind to my office to let me know.

· 178 ·

I called you, crying, from the train when I was on the way home from a catastrophic weekend with my new boyfriend. When I finally dragged in, you were waiting at my apartment door, ready to mix me a martini and listen to my sad story.

· 179 ·

If there's anything in this world
I'm sure of, I'm sure you're the
most loyal friend in the world.

· 180 ·

Feeling connected to
you makes me feel connected
to the world.

· *181* ·

We make appointments with
each other for problem-solving
sessions—how to plan our budgets,
what's the best way to get a raise,
how to reorganize the kitchen, what
to do with a child who's in trouble.

· *182* ·

You don't care if I stick
to the point or not.

· 183 ·

I don't have to watch what I say
when *we're* talking, the way I do
when I'm talking with certain other
people. And you know who I mean.

· 184 ·

When I'm sick in bed,
you call to check on
me at least
five times a day.

· 185 ·

If I make a faux pas at a
fancy dinner party, you cover
for me. Like that time I
accidentally knocked over
my glass of red wine—you
went right ahead and
knocked yours over, too.

· 186 ·

I'm the first person you
invited to join your

a. rock group

b. study group

c. playgroup

d. reading group

e. investment group

· 187 ·

You never get impatient when
we're waiting in line, so I follow
your lead and keep my cool.

· 188 ·

You like to try new things—
new music, new plays, new
restaurants, new people, new
places—and your enthusiasm
carries me along with you.

· 189 ·

I never feel competitive with you.
Well, almost never.

· 190 ·

You were *número uno* pitcher
on our softball team, so when
you tossed your wedding
bouquet in my direction,
that bouquet was *mine*.

· 191 ·

We can be completely relaxed
with each other, sitting in the
sunshine, having a glass of wine,
dipping in and out of all sorts of
topics. Now, that's not something
you can do so easily with a new
friend or even a good friend—but
you can do it with your best friend.

· 192 ·

When we were on opposing
dodgeball teams in fifth grade,
you never even *tried* to hit
me with the ball.

· 193 ·

If I go into orbit about something—
a history exam, an overscheduled
week, a humongous phone bill—
you reach right out and bring
me back to earth.

· 194 ·

You notice when I'm blue,
you ask what's wrong, and
you keep asking until
I unburden myself to you.

· 195 ·

Your special-occasion toasts
are very special. I look
forward to hearing them.

· 196 ·

Don't know how you did it
with not much more than a
piece of chewing gum and a
bobby pin, but you sure got
that faucet working again.
You're resourceful.

· *197* ·

There's always a pot of
strong coffee ready and
waiting in your kitchen.

· *198* ·

You made a list of the ten
things you love most in the
world and I was on the list.

· *199* ·

When I caught a horrible flu
and couldn't come to your big
dinner party, you packaged
up samples of each delicious
course and brought them to
me the next day. Including
a slice of your out-of-this-world
coconut layer cake.

· 200 ·

You sent your teenagers over
to help me paint my garage
when I was too broke to pay
for real painters. It came out
pretty well, and I learned
everything there is to know
about rap music.

· 201 ·

When I start acting like
a control freak, you stop me.
When you start acting like
a control freak, I stop you.
(What do we do when we *both*
start acting like control freaks?)

· 202 ·

Remember snowy winter days?
Puffy parkas zipped to our
noses, caps pulled down
over our ears, snowballs and
snow angels and snowmen . . .

· 203 ·

Remember rainy spring days?
Yellow daffodils and yellow
slickers, red rubber rain boots,
puddles we splashed in until
we were soaked through . . .

· 204 ·

Remember sunny summer days?
New shorts and new sandals,
seashells collected on the beach,
wildflowers picked for our moms . . .

· 205 ·

Remember windy autumn days?
Heavy wool sweaters, crisp new
apples and crisp new notebooks,
flying leaps into huge piles
of dry brown leaves . . .

· 206 ·

We went to a fancy restaurant to
celebrate our thirtieth anniversary—
thirty years of friendship.

· 207 ·

You're the only person in
the world who's welcome
to show up on my doorstep
at any hour of the day or
night, any day of any week.
Everyone else, call first.

· 208 ·

How many times did we walk and talk our way home from high school together, say good-bye—and then call each other five minutes later to continue the conversation? More times than I could count.

· 209 ·

Sometimes you give me tough love when I really need gentle love—but I know that's because you're worried about me.

· 210 ·

You gave me the high sign when
it was time to stop wearing

a. short shorts

b. black lipstick

c. skirts slit to *here*

d. T-shirts without a bra

e. fishnet stockings

· 211 ·

You gave me a push
to start wearing

a. colors that make me
look lively and happy
b. pants that fit perfectly
c. bathing suits that show
off my figure
d. sexy shoes
e. better jewelry

· 212 ·

You taught me the
finer points of flirting.

· 213 ·

You bring me fresh herbs
from the pots on your
sunny kitchen windowsill.

· 214 ·

Chasing after the ice cream
man was our biggest thrill on
summer days when we were kids.
Vanilla for you, chocolate for me—
or was it the other way around?

· 215 ·

There are a few dicey things lurking
in my past, and you're the only one
who knows about them—but you
don't hold them against me.

· 216 ·

I love the way you live
in the present as much
as you possibly can, treasuring
the past without clinging to it.

· 217 ·

You won't stand still for anyone
saying a mean thing about me,
and no one had better make a
crack about you in *my* presence.

· 218 ·

You took my daughter to the
office with you on national
Take Our Daughters to Work Day.

· 219 ·

We made a pact never to tell anyone about the insane pranks we pulled when we were in high school. But lately my teenagers have been giving me some funny looks. Did you spill the beans?

· 220 ·

When I hit a snag on the Sunday crossword, all I have to do is call you. What's a ten-letter, two-word phrase for bosom buddy?

· 221 ·

You asked me to make your
wedding cake the first time
you got married. The marriage
didn't last, but our friendship did.

· 222 ·

We ran the marathon together.
We made it to the finish line!

· 223 ·

Together we find beautiful
places in nature for silence,
peace, and renewal.

· 224 ·

Shopping for clothes is your
least favorite activity, but I love
it—so you make a list and
I help you get through it as
quickly as possible. Then we
reward ourselves with a
delicious dinner, for positive
reinforcement.

· 225 ·

I admire you for doing
volunteer work—dishing out meals
at the local soup kitchen on
Thanksgiving, tutoring kids learning
to read, raising money for
your favorite cause.

· 226 ·

You love to laugh.

· 227 ·

You write terrific thank-you notes. (To be honest, I've cribbed a couple of them from time to time.)

· 228 ·

You don't take your mistakes too seriously, and you don't let setbacks set you back.

· 229 ·

I appreciate the dailiness of our
relationship. We talk so often
that we don't miss a single
detail of each other's lives.

· 230 ·

You're better than a sister:
no sibling rivalry.

· 231 ·

I may screw up and
you may get mad at me,
but in the end you forgive me.
And vice versa.

· 232 ·

If I'm in the middle of
a crisis, you call me from
wherever you are—even if
you're on vacation.

· 233 ·

If I'm mopey and blue, you turn on some
music, drag me to my feet, and make me
dance until I've stomped and swiveled
my way out of my bad mood.

· 234 ·

You used to let me read your
diary when we
were teenagers.

· 235 ·

You took me for
my first professional

a. manicure

b. pedicure

c. facial

d. massage

e. all of the above

· 236 ·

Your varicose veins are
worse than mine. (But my
cottage cheese thighs
are worse than yours.)

· 237 ·

We bought our first
training bras together.

· 238 ·

We bought our first
nursing bras together.

· 239 ·

We stopped wearing
bras together. But that
didn't last long!

· 240 ·

When my husband asked you
for advice about my birthday
present, you nixed the floor
polisher and approved the pearl
necklace. I'll be forever grateful.

· 241 ·

You crocheted a soft new afghan
for my second baby. You insisted
that she should have a
keepsake all her own.

· 242 ·

You're organized at work and
disorganized at home; I'm organized
at home and disorganized at work.
Maybe that's why we're best
friends—opposites attract.

· 243 ·

My living room furniture
arrangement was
getting *soooo* boring,
so we moved it around for
hours, until it was fabulous.
Major improvement, couldn't
have done it without you.
Next time, your turn.

· 244 ·

When I was on a diet and
wobbling at the sight of the
dessert cart, you told the waiter
to take it away immediately.
I only hated you for about
thirty-seven seconds.

· 245 ·

You never told me when my
old boyfriend made a pass at
you in my kitchen, and I never
told you when yours cornered
me in the back hallway
of your apartment.

· 246 ·

You went with me to the vet
when I finally had to take my
darling old dog to be put down.
And you helped me scatter
her ashes in the park she
loved so much.

· 247 ·

I admire your ability
to change and grow.

· 248 ·

You laugh at my jokes.

· 249 ·

You always know
the right thing to say.

· 250 ·

We have regular sit-downs to
discuss our life goals and how
to implement them. So far we're
batting a pretty fair average.

· 251 ·

Remember when we were girls
and we walked home from school
together? First we walked to your
house, but we weren't finished
talking . . . so we walked back to
my house, but we still weren't
finished talking . . . so we walked
back to your house . . .

· 252 ·

Sometimes you *don't* have
time for me. That might make
me sad or hurt for a while,
but hey, you'll be back.

· 253 ·

You stand up for what
you believe and no one
can make you back down.

· 254 ·

You're an absolute stickler
for good citizenship. I don't think
you've missed an election since
you got to be old enough to vote.

· 255 ·

We live three thousand miles apart
now, but we never fail to call each
other every Sunday, and we're
just as close as we've ever been.

· 256 ·

We're both looking
forward to menopause
and relief from

a. bloating

b. cramps

c. headaches

d. PMS

e. bathroom cabinets full
of absorbent products

· 257 ·

In fourth grade you sent me a
valentine when nobody else did.

· 258 ·

You kept my houseplants
alive while I was away
for a romantic weekend
with a new man.

· 259 ·

You urge me to get
in touch with my anger.
What a relief that is.

· 260 ·

You never make
me feel guilty.
Even when I am.

· *261* ·

We joined the
same sorority.

· *262* ·

We refused to join
any sorority at all.

· 263 ·

We love a lot of the same
books and writers, and we
can't wait to share our latest
discoveries with each other.

· 264 ·

You ran every red light in town
to get us to the emergency room
when my little boy broke his arm.
And you never left my side
until the crisis was over.

· 265 ·

You always have something
good to eat in your refrigerator,
and you always feed me.

· 266 ·

You got me started taking
vitamins and calcium.

· *267* ·

I respect your ability to
differentiate quickly and
clearly between the trivial
and the important, even
in situations where it
might not be obvious.

· *268* ·

We climbed a tall mountain
together to gaze out for miles
and miles and get some perspective
on our lives. Our small worries
looked a lot smaller from up
there, didn't they?

· 269 ·

You helped me plant
243 tulip bulbs all
around my house.

500 Reasons Why You're My Best Friend

· 270 ·

You helped me sew 106 name
tapes into my daughter's clothes
before she went to sleep-away
camp for the first time. Then
you let me cry on your shoulder
when she left on the bus.

· 271 ·

Even though I hate reading
the newspaper, I'm impressed that
you read it cover to cover every day.

· 272 ·

Rudeness makes us both go
ballistic. Really, how hard is it
to RSVP to a party invitation?

· 273 ·

When we were teenagers we
spent whole days at home doing
Beauty Routines, from hair to
toenails, even when we didn't
have dates. *Especially* when
we didn't have dates.

· 274 ·

Your love for me is as
unconditional as mine is for you.

· 275 ·

You loaned me your good-luck
bracelet when I took the most
important exam of my life.

· 276 ·

Working as a duo,
we sold the most Girl Scout
cookies in the whole troop.
Go team!

· 277 ·

On class trips you always
wanted to stick close to me.

· 278 ·

Remember those few years
when we lost touch? The minute
we got together again it was as
if no time at all had passed.

· 279 ·

When I see what a wonderful mother
you are, it gives me confidence that I can
do it, too. (When I see how much time
and effort it takes to be such a
wonderful mother, I have a panic attack.)

· 280 ·

We're secret
horoscope junkies.

· 281 ·

You remember the
details (gory or exquisite)
of my latest romance
almost as well as I do.

· 282 ·

You always offer to wash
and dry the lettuce when
we're making dinner together.
Oh, how I hate washing and
drying the lettuce.

· 283 ·

When we hit thirty we
made a pact to *give* up

a. romance novels

b. staying out until four
in the morning

c. body piercing

d. bad boyfriends

e. bad bosses

· 284 ·

And we made a pact to *take* up

a. sensible eating

b. travel

c. therapy

d. belly-dancing

e. new careers

· 285 ·

When we hit forty we
made a pact to *give* up

a. ruffles

b. temper tantrums

c. elaborate dinner parties

d. blue nail polish

e. running shoes (except
when we're running)

· 286 ·

And we made a pact to *take* up

a. Italian

b. scuba diving

c. tap dancing

d. politics

e. meditation (even if the
kids keep interrupting)

· 287 ·

When we hit fifty we
made a pact to *give* up

a. earrings that dangle
to our shoulders
b. baggy sweat pants
c. boring acquaintances
d. green eyeshadow
e. complaining

· 288 ·

And we made a pact to *take* up

a. computers

b. salsa

c. spas

d. yoga

e. sexy underwear

· *289* ·

You think deep thoughts,
and you share them with me.

· *290* ·

When I was in
psychological trouble,
you insisted I get
professional help.

· 291 ·

I gave you that final push to call
the guy you'd been admiring from
afar. Okay, so it didn't work out,
but at least you dared to dream.

· 292 ·

Getting through grad school
was hard for you, but you stuck
with it and got your degree.
I'm proud of you.

· 293 ·

Sometimes, after we've
spent a few hours hashing
out a problem of mine, you'll
call me the next
day and tell me some
new thoughts you've had
about it. It warms my heart
to know you've been
thinking of me.

· 294 ·

Once a week we meet for
lunch in a quiet coffee shop or
on a park bench, and we catch
up on all the important events
of our lives. We count on that
hour or two for mental and
spiritual refreshment.

· 295 ·

I have lots of framed
photos of the people I love,
and your picture is right
there among them.

· *296* ·

The way you tackle a practical
problem is an inspiration to me.

· *297* ·

You respect my time as much
as your own: You're never late
to meet me or, if you are, you
call me on your cell phone
to apologize and let me
know your ETA.

· 298 ·

When we were eleven you
explained the mechanics of
sex to me. I didn't believe
one word you said,
but thanks for trying.

· 299 ·

Your love of flowers and
plants is delightful. I adore
being in your garden.

· 300 ·

One hug from you is worth
ten from any other friend.

· 301 ·

You gave me a subscription
to a concert series I mentioned
only once but secretly longed
to go to. You really listen
to me, don't you?

· 302 ·

You clue me in when my
husband is being insanely
unreasonable with me, like
when he wants me to iron his
T-shirts, trim the crusts off
the bread, let my hair grow
to my waist, or balance
my checkbook.

· 303 ·

You clue me in when I'm being
insanely unreasonable with my
husband, like when I want him
to mow the lawn twice a week,
give up everything fattening,
stop wearing his hair so short,
or balance my checkbook.

500 Reasons Why You're My Best Friend

· 304 ·

We went on a cruise together
and it was so much fun that I
can't remember a single moment
of actual *sleep* for seven days.

· 305 ·

Because we came of age
together and have so much
history together, our friendship
resonates with trust and ease.

· 306 ·

You stood godmother
to my first child.

· 307 ·

On Saturday and Sunday
your family comes first, so
you put your foot down about
bringing work home from
the office every weekend.
And you urged me
to do the same.

· *308* ·

You gave me permission
to stop spending so much
time in the kitchen and start
using ready-made,
packaged, store-bought

a. salad dressing

b. salsa

c. chicken broth

d. waffles

e. spaghetti sauce

· 309 ·

Your favorite maxim is
"Every problem is an opportunity,"
and you follow through on it.

· 310 ·

We have our own
best-friends shorthand
way of communicating.
You know just what
I mean, don't you?

· 311 ·

When we were teenagers
we locked arms and barreled
our way, eyes straight ahead,
past the construction workers
who whistled and yelled at us.
Now we strut past them proudly.

· 312 ·

We had a contest to see which
of us would be the first to French
kiss. Remember who won?

· 313 ·

You have a hard time making
decisions about everything from
upholstery fabric to restaurants.
I'm glad you let me help you
choose, or your couch would
still be pink and purple and we'd
have starved to death by now.

· 314 ·

You help me figure out
who my *real* enemies are.

· 315 ·

We planned your housewarming
party together. Also my birthday
party, your New Year's Eve party,
my anniversary party, your Fourth
of July party. Parties-R-Us.

· 316 ·

When you go away on vacation,
you always leave your itinerary
with me—just in case.

· 317 ·

We hiked a mountain trail
together, slept in a tent, and had an
absolutely wonderful time. And you
know how much I *hate* camping.

· 318 ·

You're a soprano and
I'm an alto, and we sing
beautiful harmony together.

· 319 ·

You got your first period
two months before me and
described it in explicit detail.
Thanks, girlfriend, *that* was
a real confidence builder.

· 320 ·

You gave me a surprise birthday
party when I turned forty, and
somehow you made sure I was
dressed in my best so I'd remember
the party with pleasure instead
of being totally humiliated by
showing up in ratty jeans, a baggy
sweater, and flip-flops.

· *321* ·

The first time I called a guy
to ask him out on a date, you
wrote the script for me and
stood right there next to
the phone until I finally hung
up and stopped hyperventilating.
Great script—I got the date.

· 322 ·

You're an early bird and I'm not,
so if I have a 7 A.M. plane to
catch or an 8 A.M. meeting to
attend, you call me on the phone
to make sure I'm up and moving.

· 323 ·

When we tool around in the car,
you always do the self-service
gas thing because I *loathe* doing it.

· 324 ·

When we tool around in the car,
we stop at every farm stand, tag
sale, Dairy Queen, fried clam bar,
and garden center we come across.

500 Reasons Why You're My Best Friend

· 325 ·

You're a firm believer in
career change: If the job isn't
working out, you find something
better and make a move.

· 326 ·

You're terrific at negotiating,
whether it's a big contract or
your five-year-old's bedtime.

· 327 ·

When we shop together, if
something looks terrible on you,
it will probably look terrific on me.
If something looks ghastly on me,
it will probably look great on you.
Now, I call that efficient.

· 328 ·

You gave me great advice
about working out: Don't
think about it, just do it.

· 329 ·

You love to do things
spontaneously—a picnic, a movie,
a trip to the country—and you
like to include me in your plans.

· 330 ·

We both started crying
at the parade. What *is* it
about parades?

· 331 ·

When we were roommates,
you used to make genuine,
slow-cooked, steaming hot
oatmeal for our breakfast.
If only I liked oatmeal . . .

· 332 ·

You tried spending a month
without TV, but in the end
you decided you couldn't
do without your favorite shows.
A woman after my own heart.

· 333 ·

You tried spending a month
without TV and you loved it.
Maybe I'll try that, too—
someday in the next millennium.

· 334 ·

You taught me the most
efficient method of packing

a. a lunch box

b. a picnic cooler

c. a suitcase

d. a car trunk

e. an itsy-bitsy evening bag

· 335 ·

I waited outside the bathroom
door with my fingers crossed
when you locked yourself in to
take the home pregnancy test.

· 336 ·

We plucked out each other's
first few gray hairs. But when
the count hit two digits, we
gave up and went directly
to the hair colorist.

· 337 ·

You have my best interests
at heart, and you never settle
for less than the best.

· 338 ·

Neither of us *dominates* our
friendship: We devote equal
time to listening and talking.

· 339 ·

You put up with my bad puns.
For this alone you deserve
a Nobel Peace Prize.

· 340 ·

You make the world's best
cup of hot cocoa. With
plenty of marshmallows.

· 341 ·

You taught me that staying
home on a Saturday night
wasn't the worst thing that
could happen to a person.

· 342 ·

I admire what a great
traveler you are.

· 343 ·

When I came home from
the hospital, there were flowers
by my bed and a freezer full
of dinners ready for defrosting.
Best of all, you were there, too.

· 344 ·

Moaning over the impossible
behavior of parents is one
of our favorite activities.

· 345 ·

We allow each other to sulk,
but not too often.

· 346 ·

You invited me to spend a week
in your best guest room when I
needed peace and quiet
to recover from a wrenching
emotional experience. Knowing
you were there for me was as
healing as the peace and quiet.

500 Reasons Why You're My Best Friend

· 347 ·

We both love spending money.

· 348 ·

We both hate spending money.

500 Reasons Why You're My Best Friend

· 349 ·

You've solved more fashion
emergencies for me than
I'd care to admit.

· 350 ·

You know how blue I get
in the depths of winter,
so you try to cheer me up.

· 351 ·

When my attic, basement, and
garage were overflowing with stuff
I didn't need, you came over and
helped me clear it all out.

· 352 ·

I got to five-pound weights
while you were still on
three-pounders, and you
congratulated me. Hey,
you'll get there soon.

· 353 ·

We snuck into a store where
they sell sex toys, just to check
out what's available. Tell the truth:
Did you go back without me
to buy something fun?

· 354 ·

I confessed to snooping
through my lover's private stuff,
and you gave me absolution.

· 355 ·

We went through the
women's movement together.
Remember sisterhood?
The Feminine Mystique?
Consciousness raising?
Equal pay for equal work?

· 356 ·

We raised daughters who
take feminism for granted.
Hallelujah.

· 357 ·

Lying about your age
makes no sense to you.
You're proud of every
year of your life.

· 358 ·

You're responsible: You started
a retirement account the minute
you had a little extra cash in
the bank. Good idea.

· 359 ·

You appreciate the less flashy
qualities of the people around
you, and you tell them so.

· 360 ·

When I'm in over my head
you try to keep me from

a. overthinking the problem

b. overworking to try to
repair the damage

c. overdoing and getting exhausted

d. overreacting to absolutely
everything

e. overeating, so I don't hate
myself in the morning

500 Reasons Why You're My Best Friend

· 361 ·

You helped me figure out a plan
for caring for my ailing parents,
and then you visited nursing
homes with me until we
located the right one.

· 362 ·

For my birthday you made
a contribution to my favorite
charity in my name.

• 363 •

Sometimes I get impatient
with you when you keep going over
and over the same old issues,
but I bite my tongue. I know
you need to work them through.

• 364 •

You have perfect intuition
for knowing when to sit back
and be patient and when
to stand up and act.

· 365 ·

Neither of us would be caught
dead wearing ultrahigh fashion.
Cool fashion, yes. Vintage fashion,
maybe. Classic fashion, sometimes.
But that weird stuff in the
glam mags? Never.

· 366 ·

You never get clingy,
but you don't mind if
occasionally I do.

· 367 ·

On Saturday mornings we leave our
kids with our husbands and spend
a few girlfriend hours scouring
antique fairs for treasures.

· 368 ·

You convinced me to hire a
housekeeper when I couldn't
handle the whole package—
husband, kids, work,
and housecleaning.

· 369 ·

You share your
newest mail-order
catalogs with me.

· 370 ·

You gave me your black
leather pants when they
got too tight for you.

· *371* ·

After we finish cringing at
whatever hideous social, business,
or family mistake one of us has
made, we remind each other
that we're only human.

· *372* ·

I love the way
you tell a joke.

· 373 ·

We bought a lottery ticket
together—and we won!
Share and share alike.

· 374 ·

The way you listen to me—alert,
attentive, intuitive, energetic,
patient, and focused—gives
me instant clarity.

· 375 ·

When my husband had to be out
of town on my last birthday, you
helped my children prepare me a
delicious breakfast in bed, and then
you stayed around to help me eat it.

· 376 ·

You're happy to meet the
new friends I make at work
because you know they're
no threat to *our* friendship.

· 377 ·

We can talk about
sex together—yours, mine,
and everyone else's.

· 378 ·

It's hard for me to hear criticism,
but you've taught me that I can
learn from it and use it to make
my life and my work much better.

· 379 ·

It's hard for me to say
I'm sorry, but you've taught
me that being in the wrong
(and admitting it)
won't kill me.

· 380 ·

Last week you dragged me, kicking
and screaming, to the playground to
swing on the swings and climb on the
monkey bars. I admit it was fun.
Okay, I admit it was a *lot* of fun.

· 381 ·

Dollhouses—oh, the hours we spent
together playing with our dollhouses,
rearranging the tiny furniture and
making up exciting stories. Whatever
happened to our dollhouses?

· 382 ·

I know, I absolutely know,
you'd whisper in my ear if

a. my mascara was running

b. my fly was unzipped

c. my blouse was fastened wrong—
you know, one button out of sync

d. my hair was sticking up in
a bizarre and comical way

e. I'd sat in something horrible
and it was all over the
seat of my pants

· 383 ·

Sometimes at ten o'clock at night
you just throw a coat over your
pj's, hop in the car, and come
over to chat for a couple of hours.
Our own private slumber party.

· 384 ·

Day care, preschool, kindergarten,
elementary school—together we've
gotten our kids through them all.
Now, heaven help us, we've got
teenagers on our hands . . .

· 385 ·

Forget the two-minute shower:
You convinced me to give myself
the luxurious pleasure of long baths
with fragrant oils, candles, soft
music. Total renewal in half an hour.

· 386 ·

You loaned me your extremely
cool raspberry-pink suede jacket
when I went to meet a new
man for the first time.

· 387 ·

You loaned me your apartment for
a rendezvous with my lover. Once.

· 388 ·

You helped me run the bake sale;
I helped you run the school newsletter.
You helped me run the campaign for
fair housing; I helped you run the church
bazaar. You helped me run the block
party; I helped you run the library
fund-raiser. That's how we do things,
and we get things done.

· *389* ·

You taught me to do a headstand.
And a handstand, a cartwheel,
a somersault, and a backbend.
Were we ever that limber?

· 390 ·

We love to sit out in the
backyard on summer nights,
wishing on the stars.

· 391 ·

We failed the math test
because we snuck out to a
dance club the night before
finals. That was very, very
bad—but wasn't the club fun?

· 392 ·

When you find a great T-shirt,
you buy me one, too.

· 393 ·

You're on friendly terms
with all your neighbors.

· 394 ·

You set a beautiful table.

· 395 ·

You gave me your treasured family
recipe for stuffed cabbage and
swore me to eternal secrecy.

· 396 ·

You bought baby clothes for your
little girl in gender-neutral colors
so you could pass them
down to me whether
I had a girl or a boy.
I had a boy.

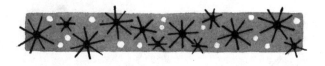

500 Reasons Why You're My Best Friend

· 397 ·

Our high school reunion was
a complete zoo. Thank heaven
we went together.

· 398 ·

We started a community theater
together. You're the director, I'm
the producer, and we positively
revel in the drama of it all.

· 399 ·

Thinking for yourself is really
important to you. But you listen
to me when I offer you the benefit
of my experience or knowledge.

· 400 ·

You helped me house hunt,
and I found the home of my
dreams. You must have
brought me good luck.

· 401 ·

You convinced me not
to waste my money
on plastic surgery.

· 402 ·

You convinced me
that plastic surgery was
worth every penny.

· 403 ·

When we were little girls
we spent hours sitting on
your bed or mine,
whispering our secrets
and giggling at everything.
We still sprawl on your bed
or mine when we need
a hefty dose of girltalk.

· 404 ·

My family didn't celebrate Christmas, so you invited me to share your family's festivities on Christmas Day. And you came to my family's Passover seder.

· 405 ·

We learned bridge together.

· 406 ·

We gave up on chess together.

500 Reasons Why You're My Best Friend

· 407 ·

We survived being roommates

a. at boarding school

b. at college

c. in our first apartment

d. on our trip to Europe

e. all of the above

Barely.

· 408 ·

Instead of throwing shoes at
the television after the nightly
news, I call you and vent till
I run out of breath. Anchor-
people drive me bananas.

· 409 ·

You have a healthy sense of
proportion about the green stuff.
If I've heard you say it once,
I've heard you say it fifty times:
It's only money.

· 410 ·

When I'm getting too thin,
you let me know. Ditto when
I'm getting too fat.

· 411 ·

You're concerned for my safety:
You insisted I meet my blind date
in a public place with plenty of
other people around, just in case
the guy was a homicidal maniac.

You're My Best Friend

· 412 ·

ou make fresh-squeezed oj
hen I come over for breakfast.

· 413 ·

I admire your ability to dream
big dreams—and try to make
them come true.

· 414 ·

We're Boomer Babes.

· 415 ·

We speak the same language.

· 416 ·

They all said we couldn't do it
and still stay friends, but we went
into business together anyway.
Our friendship survived, and
the business is solid, too.

· 417 ·

You cheered for my daughter
when she won the skating
competition, and you cheered
for my son when he had the
lead in the school play.

· 418 ·

When your husband is ill, you
share your anxiety with me.

· 419 ·

You insisted I borrow your silver
necklace—the one that looked so
good on me—for an extended loan,
and you never asked for it back.

· 420 ·

We got tipsy together
on our first bottle
of real champagne.

· 421 ·

You shared your tin
of caviar with me.

· 422 ·

You actually know
how to program a VCR.

· 423 ·

We both decided
to breast-feed.

· 424 ·

We both decided
not to breast-feed.

• 425 •

You helped me organize

a. my kitchen

b. my desk

c. my clothes

d. my life

e. all of the above

• 426 •

You sent me a
Mother's Day card.

· 427 ·

Every so often we play hooky
together—a one-day, minivacation
for the two of us: movies or
museums or shopping, and a
scrumptious dinner with a glass
of good wine. After that, we're
ready to face the world with
enthusiasm again.

· 428 ·

We went through
childhood in tandem—piano
lessons, dance classes,
Brownies, swimming lessons,
horseback riding, soccer games.
Was there anything
we didn't do together?

· 429 ·

You always give exactly
the right present.

· 430 ·

Even when other adults are in the
car, you still let me sit in the
front seat so I don't get carsick.

· 431 ·

You know how to fight fair.

· 432 ·

Sometimes I don't have time
to wrap your birthday present,
but you don't complain for
more than an hour or two.

· 433 ·

We don't hesitate to walk
out of any movie we hate.
We don't like it,
we're out of there.

· 434 ·

I love you just the way
you are and I hope
you never change.

· 435 ·

You were nice to my boyfriend
even though you didn't like him—
but when he got abusive,
you sat me down and told me
what was what. Then you helped
me get away from him and let me
stay with you until I got my head
straightened out again.

· 436 ·

When I lost one of my favorite
earrings on the dance floor,
you helped me crawl around
all those legs and feet until
we found the wretched thing.

· 437 ·

You really know how to tell
a story, without omitting
a single delicious detail.

· 443 ·

We baby-sat together so
neither of us would get scared of
anything that might happen.

· 444 ·

We have traditions we've
developed over the
years of our friendship.

· 438 ·

You have a wonderful
talent for making a room
cozy and inviting.

· 439 ·

Your recipe for lasagna
has earned me dozens of
compliments at dozens
of my dinner parties.

· 440 ·

I needed some caretaking
myself when I arrived back
home from caring for my very
sick grandmother. What a wonderful
surprise: You had changed the
sheets on my bed, put out fresh
towels, and stocked the refrigerator
with staples *and* treats.

· 441 ·

You were the first person I
showed my brand-new bicycle to.

· 442 ·

You were the first person I
showed my brand-new car to.

· 438 ·

You have a wonderful
talent for making a room
cozy and inviting.

· 439 ·

Your recipe for lasagna
has earned me dozens of
compliments at dozens
of my dinner parties.

· 440 ·

I needed some caretaking
myself when I arrived back
home from caring for my very
sick grandmother. What a wonderful
surprise: You had changed the
sheets on my bed, put out fresh
towels, and stocked the refrigerator
with staples *and* treats.

· 441 ·

You were the first person I
showed my brand-new bicycle to.

· 442 ·

You were the first person I
showed my brand-new car to.

· 443 ·

We baby-sat together so
neither of us would get scared of
anything that might happen.

· 444 ·

We have traditions we've
developed over the
years of our friendship.

· 445 ·

We borrow each other's clothes.

· 446 ·

I never would have passed

a. high school biology

b. the driving test

c. college French

d. the bar exam

e. any of the above

if you hadn't helped me.

· 447 ·

You're a great mediator
in sticky situations.

· 448 ·

Feeling guilty doesn't enter
your mind: You love to hang out
and do absolutely nothing.

· 449 ·

You have style.

· 450 ·

Cleaning up after a party—yours
or mine—is so much fun because
we dish over every last thing that
happened. And we stick with the
clean-up until every last glass
is washed and put away.

· 451 ·

We have the same discussions over
and over (your husband, my husband,
your job, my job, your sister, my sister)
but we never get bored.

· 452 ·

Sometimes you disappoint
me, but I get over it.

· 453 ·

You always have the line on who's
having a fling with whom, how long
it's been going on, and how long
it's going to last. How do you
find out this stuff?

· 454 ·

We cook double batches of dinner
food and trade dishes so we have
half the work and twice the variety
when suppertime rolls around.

· 455 ·

You save the foreign postage
from your letters to give
to my stamp-collecting child.

· 456 ·

You don't postpone your goals,
your ambitions, your promises,
or your pleasures.

· 457 ·

You have a can-do attitude.

· 458 ·

You taught me to dance the

a. waltz

b. lindy

c. frug

d. twist

e. macarena

· 459 ·

You take the most wonderful slides of
your travels, and you tell wonderful
stories to accompany them.

· 460 ·

You're an angel on my shoulder.

500 Reasons Why You're My Best Friend

· 461 ·

You urge me to be
more adventurous.

· 462 ·

You turned me on to the
time-saving culinary possibilities of
a. nonstick pans
b. the programmable slow cooker
c. the microwave oven
d. frozen gourmet dinners
e. eating out

· 463 ·

We take pride in each
other's accomplishments.

· 464 ·

You're dealing with aging just like
a pro: You love the advantages
your life experience gives you.
You're more independent than
ever. You don't give a hoot what
other people think when you know
you're right. Nothing stops you
from enjoying each moment.

· 465 ·

When I was having a meltdown
from chore overload, you tore
up my to-do list and ordered
me to bed for the afternoon.

· 466 ·

We've hit a few rough spots,
but with love and patience
we've smoothed them out.

· 467 ·

Girls' Night Out.
Enough said.

· 468 ·

Sometimes you're the most
grown-up person I know,
and at other times you're
such a baby. (You tell me
the same thing about myself.)

· 469 ·

You're good at old-fashioned
things like knitting and sewing
and baking bread.

· 470 ·

You're good at new-fangled
things like Palm Pilots and
DVDs and the Internet.

· 471 ·

You're gentle about it,
but you don't let me lie to
myself about important issues.

· 472 ·

We don't always agree—
who does?—but we've
learned to compromise.

· 473 ·

You confided you were having
problems with your husband,
and you trusted me enough
to discuss them openly.

· 474 ·

You stuck with me through
all the stages of postrelationship
nightmare: disbelief, rage, revenge,
relapse, and recovery.

· 475 ·

In the third grade you
were best friends with
another girl for six months.
Wow, I hated you for that.

· 476 ·

Sometimes we graze our
way through the supermarket
together like a couple
of hungry sheep.

· 477 ·

Secrets are secrets, and we'd
never reveal each other's.

· 478 ·

Your home is cheerful
and welcoming.

· 479 ·

I love getting stuck in traffic
with you. More time to talk.

· 480 ·

You see past the top layer
of any situation, down to
the complexities below.

· 481 ·

You place a high value
on experiences that enrich
your life, and you remind
me to do the same.

· 482 ·

We're planning to live long
enough to cast our votes for
the first female president
of the United States.

· 483 ·

When I felt like crawling into
a dark closet and staying
there for the rest of my life,
you cajoled me into going
out into the world to see
that there's life after
a bad love affair.

· 484 ·

You always carry

a. tissues

b. mints

c. an emery board

d. aspirin

e. Band-Aids

in your handbag, to cover any
emergency. You're so reliable.

· 485 ·

My husband and I desperately
needed some time alone, so
you volunteered to stay with
the kids for a whole weekend.
I think you saved my marriage.

· 486 ·

The good, the bad, and the
ugly—we've been through
it all and we're still friends.

· 487 ·

If I have to write an especially
effective business letter, I run
it past you before I send it out.
You give me good feedback.

· 488 ·

You tried to keep me from getting
homesick at summer camp, and
you never let anyone know how
much I cried the first week.

· 489 ·

You told my mom I was at
the library when she called
on a Sunday morning and
I was still out with my boyfriend.
Thank you, thank you, thank you.

· 490 ·

The two of us in the kitchen,
cooking up a storm, is just about
the most fun in the whole world.

· 491 ·

You sent me roses
when I got that
promotion and raise.

· 492 ·

You brought me a
bouquet of wildflowers
when you came back from
a weekend in the country.

· 493 ·

You can be passionate and
hotheaded—but you can be
calm and levelheaded, too.

• 494 •

I suggested that we invest in
dot-coms. We took a beating,
but you never blamed *me*.

• 495 •

When the big girls
on the playground were
picking on me, you came
running to my rescue.

· 496 ·

You held my hand when
we went into the scary, scary
fun house the first time.

· 497 ·

You taught me how to play
to win—and I taught you
how to lose gracefully.

· 498 ·

When my computer kept
crashing, you figured out
what the problem was.

· 499 ·

We've stayed up
talking all night more
times than I can count.

· 500 ·

Remember that time I waited an hour for you at the movies? You finally showed up and your excuse was pretty flimsy. There might have been a man involved. . . . Oh, well. You may misbehave, I may misbehave, but best friends accept best friends, misbehavior and all.

That's how it is.

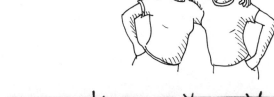